What am I? Vegetables

*Written and illustrated
by John Benzee*

What am I? Vegetables

Published by Split Seed Press; Clarence, NY
ISBN: 978-0-9997379-0-3 (hardcover)
ISBN: 978-0-9997379-1-0 (paperback)
Visit johnbenzee.com for more information

First edition

Typeset in Roboto

Publisher's Cataloging-In-Publication Data:
Names: Benzee, John, 1995— author, illustrator.
Title: What am I? Vegetables / by John Benzee.
Description: Clarence : Split Seed Press, 2017. | Series: What am I? series. | Summary: A
    series of riddles that give descriptions of various vegetables and then reveal
    their names.
Identifiers: ISBN 9780999737903 (hardcover) | ISBN 9780999737910 (paperback)
Subjects: LCSH: Vegetables—Varieties—Juvenile literature. | Riddles, Juvenile. | BISAC:
JUVENILE NONFICTION / Gardening.
Classification: SB324.B46 2017 | DDC 635--dc23

10 9 8 7 6 5 4 3 2 1

Note: This book follows the USDA, not botanical, vegetable classification

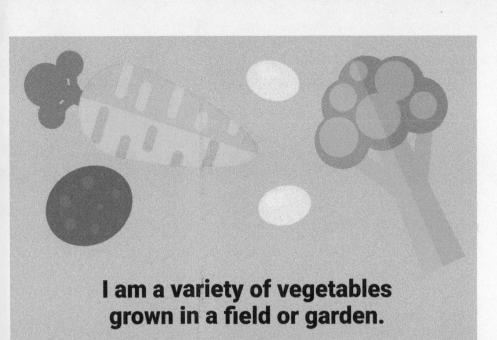

I am a variety of vegetables
grown in a field or garden.

I have some riddles for you,
curious reader,
to figure out
what types of vegetables I am.

Corn? A potato? Broccoli?

Turn the page to start guessing.

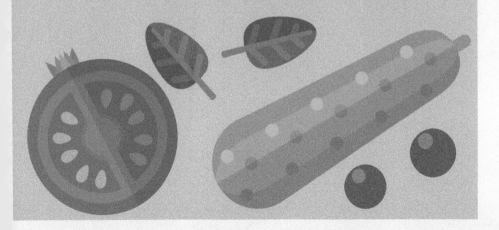

I grow upon a central stalk
Towering at six feet high,
I reach toward the sky
With big green leaves.

Rows and rows
Of sweet yellow kernels
Lined upon the cob,
Hidden from the hungry crows
Who want to peck and rob.

What am I?

CORN

I'm grown in pods
On bush or vine
With a spiraling, twisting spine,
The size of a pencil rod.

Eat me fresh
With a snap
Or open up the stringy flesh.

For kidney-shaped seeds
reside inside
Which are kept and dried,
For soups and stews or planting too
Some are even refried.

What am I?

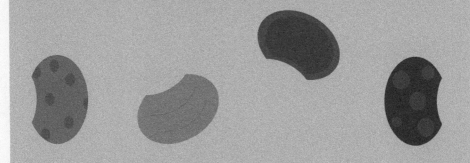

BEAN

On long prickly vines
I reach around
Seeking sunlight where it may be found

Orange flowers
peek over large leaves
To call to the busy bees.

My fruit is tender
in summer's heat,
While other times it's hard
for an autumn treat.

Many varieties grow throughout the year
As many shapes and sizes appear.

Most famous of all
Are the orange ones in the fall,
With Jack-o-lantern as my other name
Whose family is one and the same.

What am I?

SQUASH

Roots reach down
And out of sight,
While a green, leafy crown
Stretches towards the light.

I'm an orange central root
Tapered to a point
Whose sharp taste won't disappoint.
Just remember I'm not a fruit.

What am I?

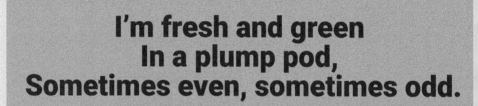

I'm fresh and green
In a plump pod,
Sometimes even, sometimes odd.

Tendrils reach out
To support and hold,
I can tolerate the cold.

For roly-poly I can be
For I like to pop free,
Because I'm a ...

What am I?

PEA

I'm very sorry
That I make you cry,
But I am a bit shy.

Purple rings keep me hidden,
But to remove my layers
Is not forbidden.

I'm a bulb
That grows underground
With a skin of red, white or brown.

What am I?

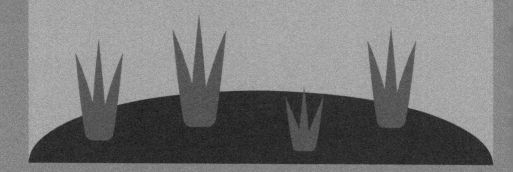

ONION

Some call me a fruit,
While others a vegetable,
I'm just content in my circular suit.

My green colored skin
Changes to red, orange, or yellow
When I'm ready and ripe within.

I can be small as a cherry
Or big as a baseball
But I'm not poisonous so don't be wary.

What am I?

TOMATO

My leafy greens
Are a nice snack
Whose growth can bounce back.

My green leaves
Are my edible part,
Shaped in a head or a heart.

I'm chopped up in salads
Or layered between bread,
I'm healthy for you to be fed.

What am I?

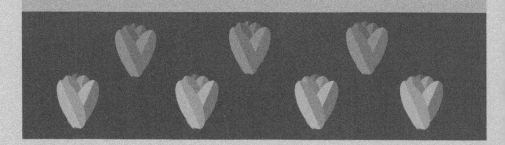

LETTUCE

I'm as cool as can be
In the midsummer heat,
My creeping vine would agree.

I can be pickled and sliced
Or even diced
When I'm full grown and ripe.

For my cylindrical shape
With bumpy skin
Is smaller than a rolling pin.

What am I?

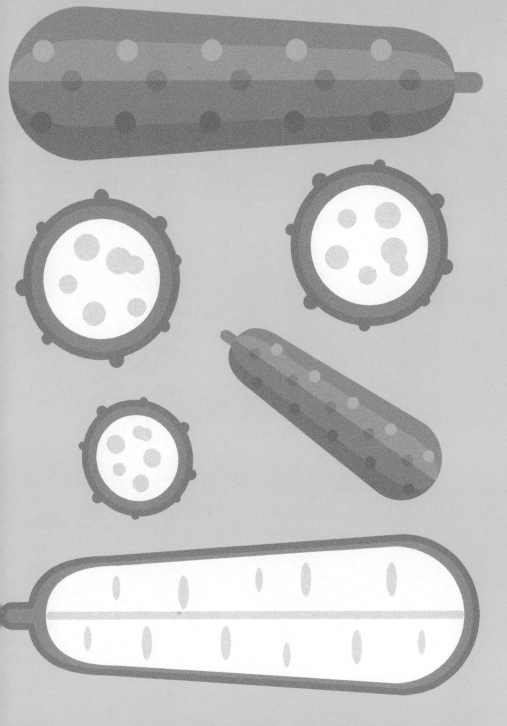

CUCUMBER

I grow underground
Where it's dark and cold,
My skin is red, brown,
and sometimes dark gold.

A sphere is my shape,
My insides pale white,
Please keep me away from the blight.

I'm boiled and baked
And also fried,
Usually served as a side.

What am I?

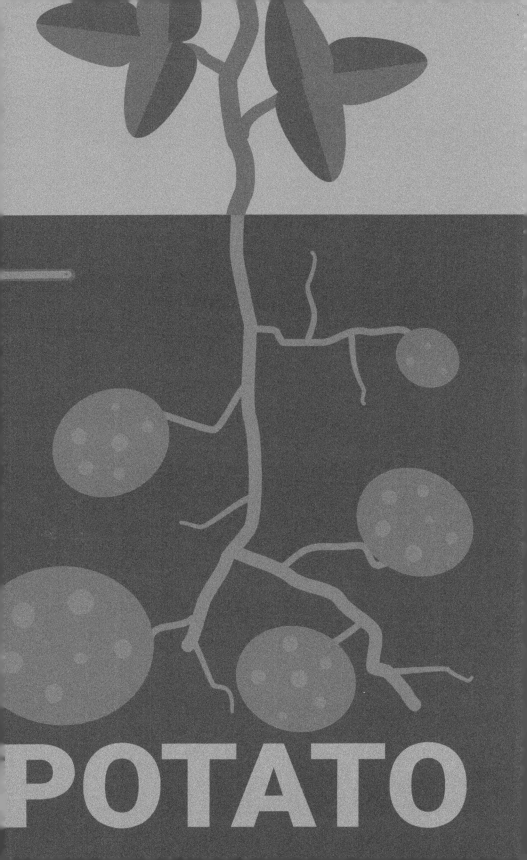

POTATO

Hot or mild
I have some heat,
I'm not always sweet.

Chili or bell
Are some nicknames of mine,
With a flavor that can make you yell.

White, green, yellow,
Purple, orange, and red,
Don't let my bright colors
cause you to be misled.

What am I?

PEPPER

Green and tall
And with a crunch,
I am perfect for lunch.

My stringy stalks,
Filled with water,
Don't like it
when the sun gets hotter.

My ribbed stalk
Leads to a leafy top,
Which are easy to cut and chop.

What am I?

CELERY

I grow under the soil
In a tight circle,
Colored red, yellow, or purple.

With a pattern of rings
My root reaches down,
While leafy tops form a crown.

My blood oozes out
When I'm cut in two,
Now you have an inner view.

What am I?

BEET

Green heads
Like a leafy tree,
Fit me perfectly.

On pale stalks
My little buds grow,
Like a bumpy meadow.

I love cool weather
All the time,
So pick me quick in my prime.

What am I?

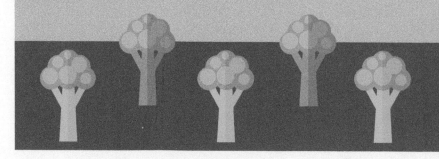

BROCCOLI

I'm a round growing root,
Down in the cool dirt,
With a quick growth spurt.

I'm planted near others,
To whom I'm a good friend,
From the pesky bugs I defend.

I'm eaten raw
With a taste that's crisp and sweet,
Sometimes with a little, spicy heat.

What am I?

RADISH

About the vegetables

 CORN grows on a tall stalk and produces cobs, which have sweet, tasty kernels.

 BEAN pods grow on a vine or bush. The pods or mature oval seeds are eaten.

 SQUASH comes in two types, summer (soft) or winter (hard), and grow on big vines. Pumpkins are a type of squash.

 CARROTS are a pointy, root crop with a crisp flavor. They come in various colors.

 PEAS grow in pods on a vine with tendrils for support. They love the cool-weather.

 ONIONS are bulbs with layers inside. They have a strong smell and can make your eyes water.

 TOMATOES are technically a fruit, but many classify it as a vegetable. Due to its red color, it was considered poisonous by early settlers.

 LETTUCE is grown for its tender leaves that come in head or loose-leaf types.

 CUCUMBERS grow on a trailing vine. They can be eaten raw or used to make pickles.

 POTATOES are underground tubers with bushy plants above ground.

 PEPPERS come in two varieties, sweet or hot. They come in a variety of colors and shapes.

 CELERY is grown for its long, crunchy stalks. It has a high water content (almost 95%).

 BEETS are grown for their spherical roots or edible leaves. Some beets ooze beet juice when cut.

 BROCCOLI contain edible heads, which are actually flower buds. It prefers cool weather.

 RADISH roots grow quickly. The plant gives off a strong scent to deter pests and is often planted with other crops.

CPSIA information can be obtained
at www.ICGtesting.com
Printed in the USA
LVHW060441181218
600845LV00015B/58/P